A Guide for Home Sellers

Valerie Hockert, Editor

Valerie Hockert, Editor
CollProf@aol.com

Table of Contents

Introduction

This book is a collection of articles that were written as individual reports for the home seller. After reading the entire book, you should be well-equipped to sell your home.

Happy selling!

Valerie Hockert

Would You Buy Your House Again?

By Mary C. McCoon

Most house hunters want to see the outside of a house before they make an appointment to see the inside. They want to drive through the neighborhood and see if it's an area they feel comfortable with and see how people maintain their homes and yards. Any real estate agent will tell you that location and first impression will sell a house. Now that you have decided to sell, you should ask yourself if your house would rate favorably on a drive-by.

When was the last time you parked your car at the bottom of the driveway or at the curb and scrutinized your property? Can you see that hanging tree limb that got struck by lightning in that storm last October? You probably duck under it every morning on your way down the drive. You've been meaning to cut it down, but haven't done it yet. How about that broken front entry light? You're used to fumbling around in the dark for your key so you haven't fixed it yet. What about the blacktop heaves in the driveway and the shrubbery you've been meaning to prune? Get these repairs done before you start to show your property. To a prospective buyer, your house represents a tremendous financial investment and probably the largest long term commitment that buyer will make in a lifetime. Cleaning up the outside is the first step toward preparing your home to show.

The following is a standard list of things to check, clean, repair and replace. Remember that you don't want to spend a lot of money in costly repairs or cosmetic remodeling. Your objective is to spruce up the outside areas to make your house and yard inviting to a stranger.

- Here are a few places to check: front entry, roof and gutters, exterior walls and siding, windows and shutters, landscaping, driveway, fencing and enclosures, outbuildings, patio and furniture, garbage cans. What do these things look like? Some may look all right to you, but on closer inspection they need help.

- How about the potholes in the driveway, broken fencing, outbuildings that are cluttered and in need of repair, garbage cans that smell, window frames that need scraping and paint, and landscaping that always needs help?

- When was the last time you cleaned out the gutters and downspouts? These are the details that a third party will immediately notice.

After you feel comfortable with the outside, start making a list for the inside and remember to use your common sense. Don't get overburdened; just do the basics.

The smell of your home is important to a prospective buyer. You are used to the smell from the garbage can, cat litter, kids' dirty sneakers, onion and fish from supper last night, and numerous other odors that may be part of your living experience. The people looking at your house know these things exist, because they have them too; but they don't want to be bombarded with these odors on a home inspection. Try baking something aromatic like an apple pie and fill the house with that homey atmosphere. If you're not into baking, then try some potpourri. The sense of smell is a strong one and can help or hinder your efforts to impress a possible buyer.

Once you set the atmosphere, you must be prepared to show every part of your house--even the closets and kitchen cabinets. Space is very important to everyone.

- Make sure all the closets are cleaned out and the contents in kitchen cabinets are arranged neatly.

- Broom closets and junk drawers should be cleaned because most people will open drawers and look into closets.

- A few standard things to check are: floors, walls and doors, windows, ceilings, lighting, bathrooms, plumbing and electric systems, furnace, basement, attic. All of these things should be cleaned and in proper working order.

- Put new, bright bulbs in light fixtures.

- Have rugs professionally cleaned and repair hardwoods if severely scratched.

- Wash windows inside and out and replace broken panes.

- Unclutter the attic and basement and make sure the toilet flushes properly and the water pressure in the sinks is adequate.

These are all small jobs that can be done in an afternoon and don't cost lots of money. As you go through the house, remember that a third party will be more objective than you.

Besides repairs, you should be aware of your personal security. You will have strangers walking through your home. Be careful. Never give out information about your personal schedule or lifestyle. Never show the house alone and always walk with the people through the house. Don't leave them alone. If they want to be alone to talk, they can go outside.

You should also be aware of any disclosure laws in your state. It would be wise to consult an attorney who specializes in real estate and find out what your responsibilities are as a homeowner. Some states have laws that require you to disclose in writing certain defects and problems.

Above all else, use your common sense in all matters. Everyone is looking for a dream home. Why not let it be your home? Once you are prepared to sell, you must decide whether or not you wish to sell it by yourself or sign a contract with a real estate agent to market your home. Either way, approach the sale of your home as a business transaction and the process will take its course.

Twelve Rules in House Selling

By Arthur F. Olds

With thousands of homes on the market and buyers becoming more sophisticated, selling your home quickly and for the right price becomes more of a challenge.

There are some basic rules of the game which you need to know to compete in the marketplace. Sight, sound and smell also has something to do with selling your home!

Pricing

The first decision is pricing.

- If your home is priced close to the market value of other homes in the area, you will have a larger pool of buyers interested in looking at your home. Buyers comparison-shop. If there are several houses comparable to yours in the area in which they want to buy, they will look to the least expensive first. They often compare differences and compromise between purchase price and items they will repair and/or replace after buying.

- Realtors experienced in the area are worth their weight in gold. Someone who is active in the area will have a bigger circle of influence over both buyers and other realtors. Hiring Uncle Jim might be nice for his ego, but if he isn't active and knowledgeable in the field, you home won't get the exposure to the buyers you need.

- The correct marketing plan is essential to selling your home. Your realtor should explain how she or he will sell your home and get it in front of the maximum number of buyers.

Exterior

How does your home looks from the street?

- Help the realtor sell your home by making sure that the yard is clean of trash, toys and weeds. Also make sure it is constantly kept mowed. You don't know what day the buyer for your home will drive by and you don't want to scare them off. Make sure the driveway surface is clean.

- If your house needs painting. A coat of paint goes a long way to increase the curb appeal of your home. If it doesn't need paint, that's O.K., too, but if the buyers looking from the curb, don't like the outside, few will even stop to look inside.

- The front door also makes a big impression on buyers. Be sure it is clean and in good working order. A coat of paint can help here, too. It seems simple, but it presents a good image to a prospective buyer.

Interior

Once inside, we again turn our attention to sight, sound and smell.

- The first thing a buyer will notice is clutter. The home will look small if you have too much furniture. It is better to put some of your furniture in storage than to have prospective buyers trying to find a path through the maze. Also, if you are in a hurry to move, you don't want packed boxes stacked everywhere. If the buyer sees this, you may be tipping your hand that you are desperate and it could be reflected in a low offer.

- The kitchen and the bathroom should be extremely clean and in working order. These are two of the most personal places in the home and many problems here are magnified by buyers.

Sounds of running water or refrigerators that sound like they are about to drive off like a diesel truck should be corrected.

- As for smell, it is ultimately important that there be no unusual odors in the home. If there are pets in the house, often the owners will not notice their odors. Unusual cooking odors sometimes linger too! Realtors sometimes have owners bake cookies on the day a prospective buyer is on the way. It creates a homey atmosphere. Your realtor should be able to tell you if there is a problem. They are not there to compliment your home, they are hired to get it sold!

Availability

Finally, your home must be available at all times.

- Realtors need access to your home at all hours. Many keep sets of keys and hang a lockbox on the front door to make the home available to other realtors. Some homeowners are uncomfortable having keys out to their homes and say that they are always home. Unfortunately, the realtor will call or come by with an interested buyer in the car and the owner has just gone to the doctor, dentist, grocery shopping or some other errand. The realtor cannot wait around and often shows an available home and sells it.

- When your home is listed for sale your realtor must know where you can be reached at all times. It is a shame if the realtor has an offer on your home just when you decide to take a weekend away and he or she can't reach you until after the offer has expired.

- Be open to different ideas when your realtor arrives with an offer. At times, buyers first offer a low price just because they have been told that a house is on the market for a higher price than the owner really wants. From a selling point, it doesn't make sense to overprice your home so no one will look at it. Don't get discouraged. Be prepared to counter their original offer. Realtors are accustomed to this.

Finally, after the offer has been accepted and you are packing to leave and making plans to move, don't count your chickens before they are hatched. Your home isn't really sold until you leave the closing table with your check in hand. There are many problems which can appear just before closing. Keep in touch with your realtor.

When you are ready to sell your home, just remember these rules for home sales and help yourself get moving!

Four Quick and Easy (and Inexpensive Ways to Prepare Your Home for Sale

By Kimberly Schilling

My brother and sister-in-law put their house up for sale in January of last year. Although the kitchen cabinets were a brownish-green, the carpets were stained and my niece had made a hole in the cellar door with her baton, they figured it was the perfect starter home and would sell quickly. But after almost five months without any offers, they decided it was time to take actions: They painted the kitchen cabinets, scrubbed the house from top to bottom, including the carpets, and replaced the cellar door. To their surprise, they sold their home within one week for the exact asking price.

This experience just shows that an appealing house, one that is neat, clean, and attractive, is always the first to go. Are you preparing your home for sale? If so, then the four following tips will help you to impress potential home buyers *without* emptying your wallet.

1. The Great Outdoors.

When a client pulls into your driveway, the first thing they see is your home's exterior. Remember, first impressions are what count the most, so be sure to put the following tips into good practice.

Exterior Lighting. Is the light over your front porch corroded from the elements? If so, replace it! Visit your local hardware store and pick something simple and elegant (brass is always a classic). If you have more than one exterior light, be sure that they all match. And, for the perfect finishing touch, buy a set of matching house numbers. Most can be easily screwed into your home's exterior walls with the proper power drill.

A Rose By Any Other Name. No, your yard doesn't need roses to be attractive. A simple row of small bushes or annuals by your walkway or next to your porch can do wonders to improve the look of your yard. No time to garden? No problem: fill a large clay or plastic pot with some top soil and a tray of pansies or impatiens. The completed arrangement can be placed on your front porch or steps. The final must: a mowed yard! Be sure to clip your grass at least one day before any clients arrive, and use a trimmer to keep all stray growth under control. Selling your home in the winter? Although you don't need to worry about your grass of any gardening, you should be sure that your driveway and walkway are clear of snow, and that they both have been sanded or salted.

2. Watch Your Step.

Flooring. Be certain to sweep and wash all floors, including those in the bathroom. Remove stubborn stains, such as scuff marks or grease, by using a scrubbing sponge and a powerful cleanser.

Carpeting. If you've had the same carpets for seven years or more, they may need a steam cleaning with any of the many machines available at your local store . For localized stains, use a spot remover, or combine ¾ cup water, ½ cup rubbing alcohol and three to four drops of a mild dishwashing liquid. Simply dip a clean scrubbing brush into the solution and scrub the stain away.

3. Rub-a-Dub Dub.

According to most real estate experts, your kitchen and bathrooms are the two focal points of your home, and so it is important to ensure that they look their best.

Kitchens. Get yourself a hot, soapy cloth and wipe down every surface in your kitchen: cabinet faces, counter tops, fridge doors, the microwave, the stovetop, and even the front of the dishwasher. If your appliances will be sold with the house, you should be sure to clean them as well. To best clean your refrigerator, empty it and use a warm, damp sponge and ordinary dish soap. The same goes for the microwave, but the stove should be put on self-clean (if you *have* it) or should be scrubbed using an oven cleaner.

Tip: If your stove is exceptionally dirty, apply the cleaner before you go to bed and remove it in the morning.

Finally, take a look at your kitchen cabinets. If they are less than appealing, you can give them a quick and easy facelift by applying a new coat of paint. Pick a neutral color that matches the kitchen (almond or eggshell look great) and be sure to remove the cabinet doors and drawers first or you'll have drips everywhere. Another quick fix: if the handles on your cabinets and drawers are outdated, then you could try replacing them (remember, stay neutral!) All you need to do is unscrew your old hardware and screw on the new hardware.

Tip: Be sure to get new handles that are exactly the same size as your old ones so that the screw holes match up.

Bathrooms. Attack all fossilized soap scum with a sponge and a heavy-duty cleanser. Scrub the bathtub with a powdered cleanser, such as Comet, to remove all dirt and hard water build-up. Once finished, dry all metallic surfaces, including the shower head and any shower door trim, with a rag for a polished look. As in your kitchen, bathroom cabinets and hardware can be touched up for maximum appeal. Even something as simple as a new mirror can change the look of the entire room. Try a beveled mirror or one in an oval or rectangular wood frame.

4. Good Scents.

Nothing is more appealing than a home with a fresh, light scent. These last two suggestions are the finishing touch to any well-groomed home.

Carpets. Cigarette and cigar smoke, cat and dog odor, even floor odor can all be hiding in your carpets. How to get rid of them? Simple! The night before potential home buyers arrive, sprinkle your carpets with a vacuum deodorizer and vacuum it up in the morning. Could your furniture use some freshening up? Then sprinkle it as well and use your vacuum's attachment.

Fresh Air. Instead of running around the house spraying air fresheners or leaving clunky bowls of potpourri everywhere, use one scented warmer in an outlet on each floor of your home. Plug-in air fresheners are attractive and virtually unnoticeable.

So, there you have it. Four simple ways to beautify your home that should help your sale along quickly *and* keep you from emptying your bank account. And, after all is said and done, you may even decide to stay in your new and improved home yourself!

What about Windows?

By Marcia Currier

Selling a house is a monumental task, one that some compare to the excruciating experience of pulling teeth. Dread and anxiety can be experienced when putting a house on the market. However, you can do some things to help sell your house with less panic and stress.

Purchasing a home is probably one of the biggest decisions you will ever make. A home is not merely a shelter; it becomes a part of you and your family, reflecting your interests and lifestyle. Let us not forget the old adage, "If you can't go anywhere else, you can always go home."

There are many factors to consider when buying a home, and they should all be taken into account very seriously. This article will tell you what to look for in what can be one of the major expenses in a home...windows.

What to Look for in New Construction

Insulated glass is your best bet for energy conservation. The selling feature of these windows is double panes of glass with an airtight seal, thus eliminating the need for traditional storm windows.

Tip: Check the date on insulated glass. It is located on the metal strip between the panes. This is important, as the builder may have used older products that have been languishing in a warehouse for a few years and the airtight seal may have broken. An indication of a broken seal is condensation within the two panes of glass. It can't be repaired; it has to be replaced. Large "picture" windows should be checked for a rainbow effect in the glass (which is one rainbow you don't want to see). This is caused by the two panes collapsing on each other, and requires replacement. These problems are not common in new construction. Most reputable builders use new products reflecting the latest technology. After all, they want you to be happy with your purchase and keep their name in good standing.

Checklist for New Construction

- Screens, grills, locks, operational hardware

- Warranty on windows

- Weather-stripping*

- Smooth operation

- Tilt-out vs. stationary

- Vinyl-clad vs. paint

A properly weather-stripped window unit is fitted at the top and bottom sash as well as at the meeting rail:

Considerations in Older Construction

The purchase and renovation of an older home can be challenging and rewarding as you see your long hours of labor pay off in true uniqueness. Many older homes have some really spectacular windows in an array of designs and angles. Unfortunately, years have usually taken their toll on the older homes and there are many points to consider with this type of purchase.

The foremost pitfall of older construction is rot. Check windows outside where the casing meets the sill. This is the most commonplace for rot to start, and if you find it there, chances are it has spread to the side jambs as well. If the house is surrounded by excessive, overgrown shrubbery, check the wood behind it, as it too may have fallen victim to the dreaded rot.

Years ago, weights and cords were used as window balances. This caused loose-fitting windows with large pockets on either side of the frame where these weights were concealed. Because the weights needed space in which to operate, there was no way to insulate this area, resulting in tremendous heat loss.

Another consideration is the old Philadelphia-style window which has no parting bead and no way to weather- strip at the meeting rail in comparison to Boston and New York styles.

Checklist for Older Construction
- Evidence of termites (fine sawdust around foundation at sills)

- Evidence and/or extent of rot

- Storms and screens

- Locks

- Deteriorating glaze

- Peeling paint

- Cracked or broken panes

- Loose-fitting sash

- Type of balances used (i.e.: weights and cords)

The more deterioration you find, the costlier your repairs and/or replacements will be. However, knowing what you're dealing with from the beginning is a lot better than several big financial surprises when you haven't anticipated them.

Tip: Many older homes have stained glass windows. If the seller is using these as a feature, be sure to inspect them carefully. Their condition could affect the price of purchase. Original stained glass windows were made without modern technology. As a result the lead cane used to join the sections may be weathered and separated. This can cause water damage to the window, as well as chipped or cracked glass. Stained glass windows are beautiful, but they can be costly to replace. Again, better to know what you're getting into.

Windows are a very important feature of any home. They illuminate and bring life to a room. House plants thrive in their light and help purify the air. They allow natural ventilation when it's warm, and when the cold wind is blowing, they allow you to look out on the storms from the warmth and comfort of your home.

Five Tips that Can Help in Selling Your House

By Sharon Spivey

Selling a house is a monumental task, one that some compare to the excruciating experience of pulling teeth. Dread and anxiety can be experienced when putting a house on the market. However, you can do some things to help sell your house with less panic and stress.

No one questions the power of first impressions. "Curb appeal" or that first look, the first moment your house comes into view is important. It is the start of a favorable or not-so-favorable attitude. It can stop the car or cause it to keep going without even so much as a second glance. But, like a good novel, there has to be something substantial beyond the first page. Something has to hold and extend the buyer's interest beyond the front lawn and that first sight.

The idea of "home appeal" can sell your house by distinguishing it from the numerous others in the neighborhood with "For Sale" signs parked out front. "Home appeal" is that ambiance that says this was your home and it feels as if you cared and took a great deal of interest in preserving it. "Home appeal" is the wind that fans the flames of imagination as prospective buyers tour your home and dream of making it their own.

A little creativity and resourcefulness can give your house "home appeal" and make it attractive enough to entice buyers to take a second look. During that time, they can ask questions as to why the house is worthy of their time and money.

There are five inexpensive things you can do to separate your house from the other house choices available in your neighborhood. These five tips will help give your house the appeal it needs to sell itself.

Tip #1: Clean out the corners in every room. Cleaning is usually the first topic of discussion between an agent and a seller. The simple act of clearing all the corners in your house opens up the space and gives the buyer a sense of more room. The optical illusion doesn't change the dimensions of the room or the available living space in the floor plan, but it does create a feeling of space and openness.

Tip #2: If the walls still need a little something extra after the painting is finished, stencil instead of papering. Wall paper can be expensive and a pain in the neck if you are not adept with long, sticky, strips of patterned paper and straight edges. Stenciling is much more cost-effective and doesn't require the skill that papering does. A brush, some stenciling paint, and a precut stencil is all that is needed. Varying degrees of skill result in different styles. A smudged design? No problem! It's not a mistake. Rather, it becomes a primitive or rustic design.

You don't have to stencil a complete room. An area of interest will suffice. A friend who recently sold her house stenciled a row of birdhouses and flowers along a kitchen counter. It was one small detail, but it became the topic of conversation when the buyer came back for a second look.

Tip #3: If you do nothing else, create an appealing entrance to your house. That doesn't mean you have to go out and purchase a new, expensive, oak door. All you need to do is repaint, repair, or refresh the old one. If it is plain and doesn't command much attention, add a spark by adding extras on your foyer or porch. Add plants or ornamental designs, but not too many. One dramatic piece will do the job. The entrance to my friend's house already had an ordinary rock garden to one side of her front door. She weeded the bed. Then, she added a small birdbath and one yellow rose bush. It was attractive and provided a pleasant impression as the buyer approached the entrance to her house.

Tip #4: Clean out your closets. Even if they are small and lack the room and organization of newly constructed units, straighten your shoes. Make sure no heaps of shoes are piled over to the side. Tidy up your hangers. Don't leave shirts and blouses hanging half-on and half-off the hangers.

Make the most of what closet space you have. Closets are a huge selling feature and often sellers give up on their closets because they don't have all the space and racks of the newer ones. Don't! Straighten! Once again, tidiness and organization create a sense of space even when little is available.

Tip #5: Give your house personality. After removing the clutter and packing up the unnecessary items, showcase your personality. Use your house as one gigantic display case. By doing so, you can bring your house to life by creating a sense of energy and vitality. Families live in houses. Display how you lived quite happily in your house. Collections, whether small or large, expensive or inexpensive, give personality to the house through the interests of the homeowner. They foster an inviting, relaxed atmosphere. My friend left her collection of cartoon memorabilia out for buyers to see and discuss and linger over. The longer they stayed, the more opportunity she had to sell the outstanding features of her home.

Putting a "For Sale" sign on your front lawn means getting your house ready for inspection by others. The scrutiny and microscopic examinations can cause many sleepless nights. Buyers can be meticulous and obnoxious about the quality and state of your home. It is a trying time. Nonetheless, there is help to overcome some of the anxiety.

In the end, my friend sold her house to a young couple in less than three months. It was an ordinary house, not unlike others on the same block for sale. The difference was she used the five tips to convince the buyers that her house was different than the one they wanted to buy.

Windows Help Sell a Home

By Paula Copeland

If you are marketing your home, don't underestimate the impact windows make on a prospective buyer. You have one chance to make a first impression and nothing says home like the sun streaming through a clear window on a beautiful day.

Unfortunately, a closer look at your windows may reveal more to a serious home buyer than what the weather is like outside. As such, you should take some time to make a careful inspection of your windows and complete minor fix-ups before listing your house. If there are no obvious problems like cracked and broken panes, most repairs and minor improvements are fairly inexpensive and require tools and materials most homeowners already have on hand.

First impressions begin outside, so take a walk around the exterior of your home and look at the windows from a home buyer's point of view. Are the windows hiding behind overgrown bushes, trees, or vines? Windows aren't only functional; they are designed to add grace and personality to the exterior of a home. Branches scraping on panes and frames could cause unsightly scratches and clinging vines may damage the seals. Trim back overgrown landscaping and bring your windows out into the open.

Now that things are out in the open, carefully inspect around each window frame. Remove old caulk that's no longer doing its job. Fill gaps, cracks or holes between the frame and the exterior wall with fresh caulk. Your local hardware store will have a variety of reliable brands of exterior latex and silicone caulks. Check wooden frames for any signs of rot and repair or replace as needed. Exterior accent shutters should be securely fastened to the wall and in good repair. Remove peeling paint with a scraper or a stiff brush and apply a fresh coat of exterior latex paint for a clean, fresh appearance.

And don't forget the screens! Shabby screens make a house appear neglected. Most local hardware stores will replace torn screens for a very reasonable price. Screens with frames so bent they don't sit snugly in their tracks should be completely replaced. Take down each screen and give it a good scrubbing on both sides with soft brush and mild detergent. Spray it off and let dry before replacing.

Now go inside and draw back those drapes, pull up the blinds, and fling back the shutters! If you find yourself peering through a fog, and you don't live by the ocean, then moisture is trapped between the panes of your double-paned windows. This is definitely not the kind of impression you want to make. Call local glass companies and get estimates on replacing the panes. Shop around, but get the best you can afford. It'll pay off in the long run.

Next, open and shut each window. Does it open easily, slide smoothly, and shut tightly? Are the tracks full of dirt and bug bodies? Do the locks shut easily and securely? Is weatherstripping in good shape and forming a tight seal? This includes sliding patio doors. You can purchase replacement rollers for sliding glass doors so they'll glide quietly with little effort. remember that people will be test driving these windows. Make it a pleasant journey.

Window treatments complement and set off windows, so take a few minutes to look them over. Traverse and curtain rods should be fastened securely to the walls. Traverse rods should pull open smoothly and glide completely shut. Blinds and shutters should also be in good condition. Dirt dulls window treatments, so vacuum drapes and thoroughly dust blinds. Wooden blinds with a natural finish could benefit from a lemon oil treatment to highlight their natural warmth.

Be sure to examine around each window. Normal expansion and contraction of the frames can cause minor cracks at the corners and around the sides. You can use a quality painter's latex caulk to seal these minor cracks. Top it off with a fresh coat of semi-gloss interior latex paint for a bright finish. Semi-gloss paint will stand up better to future cleanings.

Speaking of cleaning, make your windows sparkle inside and out. This is the easiest and least expensive way to improve any window.

Now, you can step back and enjoy the view. The view of impressed home buyers, that is!

Increase Your House's Appeal with Homespun Touches

By Ella Robinson

When preparing a house for sale, people often get out the paint brush, buy new carpet, add a new roof, clean closets, and on and on. However, many sellers overlook a key ingredient—creating appeal.

Purely by accident, I stumbled upon this essential fact of selling. When we put our first house on the market, we had an enthusiastic agent. He pointed out the best features of our house to a parade of people seemingly day and night. However, his first attempts to attract one couple to the garden room at the front of the house or the gas log fireplace in the living room were unsuccessful. The potential buyers were propelled by their sense of smell, straight through the garden room, past the dining room, and into the kitchen where a ham was baking in the oven.

Our senses have powerful control over us. Even people who are patient and deliberate in their purchases can be influenced by their senses. In other words, when the senses are happy, a person is happy. The smell of ham wafting through the house appealed to the couple's senses and perhaps brought good memories of their childhood. Just by adding a few items to your decor to attract the sense of sight or touch or by leaving a plate of fresh baked bread on the countertop to attract the senses of smell and taste, you can add appeal to your home and perhaps encourage prospective buyers to see your house as a home.

Try a few of these suggestions. For a small amount of effort and little cost you can add sensory appeal to your home and attract the attention of potential buyers.

Bedrooms

1. Place a rag doll or teddy bear in a child's rocking chair.
2. Toss a jump rope or a well-worn doll on the bed.
3. Hang a model airplane from the ceiling.
4. Turn on a toy train set.
5. Open the lid to a toy chest.
6. Leave some teenage magazines or comic books on the bedside stand.
7. Turn the computer on and leave a book open beside it.
8. Use a quilt for a bed throw.
9. Turn on a lamp.
10. Have a radio playing softly.
11. Turn on the ceiling fan.
12. Use table runners and doilies for the tops of dressers and cabinets.
13. Display wedding photos and snapshots of special family events.

Bathrooms

1. Hang a whimsical shower curtain liner, and let it peak out, almost as a secret.

2. Light a scented candle.

3. Put out a bowl of shaped guest soaps.

4. Use a thick, soft rug for the floor

5. Put a large pot of blooming violets on a shelf. (Provided they have ample light, violets grow well in a steamy bathroom.)

6. Hang colorful guest towels.

Hallways

1. Display old, black-and-white photographs of your grandparents, uncles, aunts, and cousins.

2. Hang fancy glass or pewter wind chimes from the ceiling.

3. Place a small decorative table under an ornate mirror.

4. Add a bright table covering to a small round table.

5. Have a delicate wooden chair in the corner.

6. Fill a candy bowl and place it on a small table.

7. Place a holiday decorations such as a cornucopia, pine cones, or a basket full of Easter eggs on a table.

Kitchens

1. Boil simmering spices on the stove.

2. Bake gingerbread or an apple pie.

3. Place a rocking chair and a braided rug in one corner.

4. Have a cookbook open on a countertop.

5. Place one or two of the children's drawings on the refrigerator. (Don't make it cluttered!)

6. Hang a sun catcher in a window.

7. Hang decorative dishtowels, pot holders, and oven mitts.

8. Set decorative cookie jars or teapots on shelves or countertops.

Family Room

1. Place a basket of magazines and/or newspapers beside a comfortable chair.

2. Place a sewing or knitting basket near another chair.

3. Open a colorful coffee-table book on the coffee table.

4. Leave out current magazines.

5. Place family pictures on tabletops, in shelves, and on walls around the room.

6. Use lots of throw pillows of different sizes and shapes.

7. Toss an afghan or decorative blanket over the back of a chair.

8. Have a bowl of wrapped snack crackers, chips, etc., on a table in a corner of the room.

9. Make collages of your favorite cartoons, frame them, and hang them on the wall.

10. Place pots of live plants in different sizes and shapes around the room.

11. Turn on track lighting or lamps.

Living Room or Dining Room
1. Display unusual artifacts or items with a history that would be good conversations starters.

2. Decorate with leaves and flowers from the yard.

3. Set out polished silver trays or crystal bowls.

4. Place large plants such as ficus or citrus trees in a corner.

Throughout the House
1. Use potpourri, scented oils, and sachets, but don't mix odors and overdo.

2. Place cut flowers in pretty vases or unusual containers. When possible get the flowers from a bed or garden outside, and draw that to the attention of potential buyers.

3. Turn on ceiling fans or gas logs. Light a fire in a fireplace or have a wood-burning stove going, when appropriate. This will help potential buyers see how well the equipment works as well as create a comfortable atmosphere.

As you are getting out the paint brush, buying new carpet, and adding a new roof, don't forget to add comfort to your home. A few homespun touches to appeal to potential buyers'' senses will go a long way. After all, an agent can point out the best features of the house but you are the one who can show potential buyers the house is really a home.

Tips to Impress Buyers: Little Touches Make the Difference

By Karen Davison

Imagine for a moment that great-aunt Sally has decided to visit and you haven't seen her since 1975 at your college graduation. Ort the team from the office is holding this Saturday's meeting at your house. Or you've just won a good-neighbor award and the local newspaper wants to photograph you in front of your house.

Suddenly you see your house in a new light. How long have those weeds been poking through the cracks in the sidewalk? When did the fence fade to gray? Didn't you mulch the flower beds just last month?

When important people come to your home, you begin to notice things that usually fade into the background of everyday life: A tilting mailbox, peeling paint, a patchy lawn, overgrown trees and shrubs. All of these things make an impression on first-time visitors. And potential buyers are perhaps the most important first-time visitors you'll ever have, at least from a financial perspective.

"You never get a second chance to make a good first impression," says Brian Begley, a realtor with ERA The Polo Group, Inc. In Tampa, Florida. "You want to make your home as inviting as possible for potential buyers."

Where to Begin?

Let's start with the outside.

"We're talking about curb-appeal," says Begley who advises sellers to drive up to their own homes and park across the street. Try to look at your house as if you have never seen it. Does it look like the kid of home where you would like to live?

Is the lawn manicured? Are the shrubs trimmed? Make sure to re-sod bald spots on the lawn. Spread fresh mulch around the shrubbery. Trim low-hanging branches from trees. Shape up those azalea bushes. The landscaping is the first time buyers will observe, and you want them to see landscaping that says this is a neat and well-cared-for home.

Obvious repairs needs to be made. Paint the house if it needs it. Replace any rotted wood under the eaves and around windows. Buy a new mailbox. Repair, replace or paint the fence. The few dollars you spend in repairs will be recouped easily in the selling price, and will give the buyer less leverage in negotiations.

Sometimes all that's necessary is a little elbow grease. Clean gutters. Make the windows sparkle and wash the screen. Get rid of that oil stain in the driveway. A little sweat equity can pay off in the long run.

After buyers have made it to the front door, some simple, inexpensive touches say "welcome." Paint the front door, buy a new doormat and place flowers by the door. Add a seasonal wreath. Make sure the doorbell works and the doorway is brightly lit. All of these things say, "Come on in. We're glad you came."

Insider's View.

Okay, your buyers have made it inside the house and seem pleased. What about the inside? Begley recommends that your home appeal to buyers' senses/

The Eyes Have It. Bright rooms beckon visitors to enter and imagine the possibilities for their own families. Light brings the illusion of space: well-lit rooms appear larger. And rooms filled with sunshine say you have nothing to hide. Buyers want to see nooks and crannies and everything between.

So. Open those blinds and turn on lamps everywhere—even in closets. If the weather is hot as September in Tampa, you may have to forego lighting a fire in the fireplace. But if there is a nip in the air, a crackling fire adds a nice touch.

Avoid clutter at all costs. When people see clutter, they think small. Put away your matchbook collection and grandma's miniature dolls. Keep counters and tabletops clean. Remove one or two pieces of furniture, if possible, from rooms that have that crammed-in look. Clean out and organize closets to give a roomy affect. And don't stack items in closets—stacking makes the closets look smaller.

Buyers want to see sparkle everywhere, particularly in the bathroom and kitchen. Polish fixtures. Scrub away mildew and replace grouting. Wax the floors until they shine. Clean all mirrors. Bathrooms and kitchens are big selling points, but don't forget the rest of the house. Have the carpets throughout the house professionally cleaned. And dust-free furniture is a given.

Nothing Says Loving. Nothing will send your buyers down memory lane faster than the smell of baked goods wafting toward them as they enter your house. Chocolate chip cookies are favorites and evoke happy thoughts of grandma and family. So bake cookies the day of open house.

If baking isn't your strong point, place a scented ring on a light bulb. Begley says vanilla and orange scents are most appealing. Or burn some candles. Besides the pleasant fragrance, candles add visual life to rooms.

Silence Isn't Always Golden. Background music will add an ambiance to your home and will cover the silence that makes some people uncomfortable. Instrumental music should add the right touch, allowing conversation between buyers while encouraging browsing.

And Finally.

One last thing. Remember those chocolate chip cookies? Place a plate of those in the kitchen next to a pitcher of tea or juice. Add a small dish of mints in the living room. You want buyers to linger long enough to appreciate all your home has to offer. By sprucing up your home and appealing to buyers' sense, you have a much better chance of creating pleasing experiences for buyers. And a much better chance of making that sale.

A Seller's Checklist

By Rick Brook

Once you have decided to sell your house you need to start looking at your home from a different point of view. You will want to sell it quickly and as close to the asking price as possible. Little items you see every day that do not really bother you, may give a future buyer a point to dicker on. The more little things that are taken care of prior to putting it on the market, the better off you will be.

Outside the House

Let's start from the beginning to take a look at what the buyer might see. Go outside and take a good look at your house.

Yard & Landscaping

- How does the yard look? Neatly trimmed, well-watered lawns help a lot.

- If you have flower beds, are they weeded and neat?

- If you have shrubs, are they trimmed?

- Look at your sidewalk. If there are cracks or holes, these can be repaired very easily and will improve appearance greatly.

- If you have a fence, is it in good repair? If it is wood, are there any broken or missing pickets? Does the fence need to be painted or to be treated with a wood preservative?

- Look at the trees. Do they need to be trimmed?

Foundation

Walk a little closer to the house: Look at the foundation.

- Are there cracks that should be filled and repainted?

- If you have siding, are all pieces firmly fastened to the house? Are there pieces missing?

- If the house is painted, are there bare places where the wood underneath shows through? (This could be a problem with many lending institutions.) You could get by with a single coat of paint, but two is better.

Exterior

- Look at the rain gutters. Are they firmly attached to the house? Are they clean and all joints caulked properly?

- Look at your windows and storm windows. Are they properly caulked and clean? Are the screens all there, and do they fit tightly? As time goes on, we sometimes miss these things.

- Little things like painting the vents and vent pipes will also add to the appearance of the house. Making sure that all these areas are properly caulked with proper roof caulking, will also show that the rood has been properly maintained.

- How does your roof look? It may be a good idea to have a local contractor do an inspection. This will inform you whether or not there are any problems and aids in showing the buyer that the house is a good investment.

- If you have a chimney, has it been cleaned recently? You might also want to call the local fire department and ask for an inspection. If the chimney is brick, is the mortar in good condition, and are all the bricks secure?

Inside the House

Now let's go inside your house.

Doors

- How do your doors look? Is the weather stripping in place and in good condition?

- Is the storm door completely there and closing properly?

Windows, Floor, and Furniture

Your house should be bright when the potential buyer enters your home.

- Raise your blinds, and make sure your windows are clean.

- The carpets should be clean and floors should be waxed.

- The furniture should be dusted and clean.

Walls

- If you have paneling, it should be oiled or polished.

- If the walls are painted, the paint should look new.

- Wallpaper should be glued down in areas where it has come loose. The baseboards should be repaired and clean.

- Make sure the ceilings are clean and free of stains.

Kitchen and Bath

The kitchen and bathroom will probably be two of the most important rooms you need to prepare. Make sure that these rooms are very clean. Burning scented candles or potpourri will enhance the room's appearance.

- Stand back and really look at these rooms. Do they have a clean attractive look?

- Be sure to have appliances clean and gleaming.

- If the sinks are stainless steel, make sure they shine and are not cleanser-streaked; if they are porcelain, make sure they are shiny.

- Make sure the exhaust fan works properly and the screen is clean.

- Putting an orange in the garbage disposal will freshen the odor that comes from there.

- Look at your kitchen cabinets and drawer fronts. Clean and polish them and make sure that they open and close properly. Clean the cabinets and drawers.

- Everything in the bathroom needs to sparkle.

- The grout on the tile is an area that may require attention. Remove all stains. There are a lot of products on the market now that will solve this problem for you should you need one.

- Check the bathroom towel racks. Make sure that they are shiny and well attached to the walls.

The Final Check

Walk through your home once more. Look at everything with buyer eyes.

- Check your switch plates. Are they all there and clean?

- Look in every corner of the house.

- Look for cobwebs or anything that would draw your attention if you were looking to buy.

Most of the items listed could be fine, but it never hurts to look at things a bit closer. A little time and money spent at this stage will only help you in the long run. What you invest now will put more money in your pocket in the future. A good handyman will be able to assist you in any project that you need assistance in.

Now that you have your house ready for sale, you may choose to sell it yourself, or use a realtor.

Overpricing Can Be a Dangerous Thing

By Terri DeGezelle

"Bob, if we just set our asking price a little higher we may have money left over to pay off a few of our bills," Mary said to her husband.

This is a common thought when putting your home up for sale. Several more thousand dollars is a temptation that some sellers can't resist, but overpricing can be a dangerous situation to get into. The housing market does not take into consideration your personal needs. The market is driven by supply and demand.

Home buyers are some of the most educated buyers there are and for good reason. Their home is probably the largest purchase they'll make in their lifetime.

Real estate companies, like any other business, have set budgets for their advertising dollars. They are more apt to spend those dollars on homes that are priced appropriately, sell more quickly, and generate more sales and revenue for the firm.

Realtors may use the overpriced home as an example to impress the buyers in regards to another piece of property that may be comparable to yours but at a lower price.

It will be noticed by a buyer if a home has been on the market for an extended period of time: they will usually contribute it to overpricing.

Buyers and realtors are like the rest of us and have busy schedules. Realtors will often avoid homes that are overpriced and show their clients only the best options. The National Association of Realtors' research show that 64.6% of buyers are working through agents versus newspaper ads, signs or personal contracts. With this kind of statistics you want the realtors on your side. Realtors will more often show a home that is realistically priced than one that is substantially above market value.

The market exposure of your home is directly related to the price of your home. One study showed that 10% of buyers will look at a home that is 15% above the market value while 60% will view a home that is priced at market value and 90% of buyers will look at a home that is 15% below the market value.

The N.A.R. conducted a survey that indicated that, as the length of time a home was on the market increased, so did the margin of difference between the asking price and the selling price. In other words, if your home was reasonably priced and sold in less than four weeks, you got an average of 0.8% more than the asking price. The longer your home is on the market, the more the selling price goes down. For example, if your home has been on the market three to 24 weeks, the selling price is, on average, 6.4% below the asking price. For those homes on the market for more than 24 weeks, the selling price is an average of 10% below the asking price.

If your job has you transferring to another city, an overpriced home can result in monetary loss to you and your family, the inconvenience of showing your home to people just looking, the time and effort spent on making your home presentable for each showing, and delay in your transfer.

Many times there is a contingency when selling your home. If the price is a hurdle for buyers, you may have a monetary loss, lose an opportunity to make a purchase of your own, or have the responsibility of making two mortgage payments at once.

Home sellers believe that, even if their home is overpriced, the buyers can always make them an offer. Buyers will examine the entire market and often not even bother with a home that is overpriced. They just don't want or need the hassle in their life.

It may be hard to believe, but overpricing may eventually even help the buyer. When buyers find out that your home has been on the market for an extended period of time, they will assume that either there is something wrong with your home or that you are getting desperate to sell your home for a price lower than the market value.

Financing may present a problem when the buyer goes to get a loan on an overpriced house. Mortgage companies and banks will not finance a loan when the selling price is over the appraised value.

So if overpricing can be dangerous, how do you come up with the best asking price for your home? Visit with your realtor and ask him/her to perform a CMA (Competitive Market Analysis) on your home. This is a service that real estate companies offer as a customized comparison of recent "solds," "expireds" and "on the market" homes that are comparable to your home. After you have learned all you can about the fair market value of your home, you may still have questions to ask your realtor. Pricing your home at a realistic price that buyers are willing to pay will produce a positive outcome for all involved. The benefits will be fewer inconveniences, an earlier sale, and a greater return on your money with a much sooner turn-around time.

Choosing a Good Real Estate Agent

By Regina Ali

A buyer or seller of property should take the time to carefully select a real estate agent. The decision to buy or sell property is a decision that has both financial and personal effects on your life.

Some people make less than a handful of real estate transactions in a lifetime. This is not a decision that should be made without careful consideration. Too often, people feel that all real estate agents are the same.

Many people do not realize the difference a good real estate agent can make. If you do not know a good agent, it is worth your time to do your homework and find one!

This doesn't mean you should hire the first stranger who says "I'll sell your home. I'm an agent!" Just because a person took the test to be a real estate agent doesn't necessarily mean he knows how to buy or sell real estate.

Some real estate agents are new to the business. The only time this might be to your advantage is if you are sure he is really motivated! He still has a lot to learn and you might not want to be the person who teaches him his job.

You want a real estate agent who is personable and caring. There is nothing worse than a "big bully" pushing his way through your transaction. (Of course, if you are selling rather than buying, having a "pushy" agent seems to have its advantages.)

Your best real estate agent is going to be a friend or business associate who knows and cares about your needs. But before considering a friend you should keep in mind that he is human. You need to decide if this person would always look after your best interests.

Some people think they should not do business with friends. In this case, it is not true. A true friend is going to be there for you when you are unable to represent yourself. A friend could obviously represent you much better than a stranger.

If you don't have a friend who is a real estate agent, you should consider a business associate. If you know someone who is a real estate agent, it would probably be in your best interests to work with him/her, as he/she would be more likely to care about your personal needs than a complete stranger.

Ask a few friends if they know any real estate agents, if you don't know one yourself. The agent with the best recommendation is a good person to consider if you need a real estate agent.

If you are still unable to locate a real estate agent, it's time to go out and meet a few. Make a few phone calls (at this point you really don't have a choice but to use the yellow pages) and set up at least three appointments with agents whom you have spoken with on the telephone. If you didn't have a good feeling about them on the telephone (or if they didn't seem to understand your needs) scratch them off your list!

After meeting with at least three agents, decide if there was one that made you feel most comfortable. Did the agent seem to really care about your needs? If you are unable to feel comfortable with at least one of the agents (or you are not sure whether or not you're comfortable with them) don't hesitate to call three more agents. Remember, you are the person hiring them.

Call the Better Business Bureau to be sure the agent (or business) does not have a lot of complaints against them. If you find an agent with a bad reputation, you should definitely choose someone else on your list.

It is very important that the real estate agent has a good reputation. You want to work with someone who is honest. There are a lot of good real estate agents out there. By law, they must have good ethics. However, it never hurts to have an agent who really seems to care about your individual needs.

You must remember when hiring an agent that you are committed to work with that person for a minimum amount of time. If you are selling a property, you will be expected to honor a written contract usually allowing the agent all rights to sell the property. If you do not cooperate with the agent (even though he should be cooperating with you), he can sue you for breaching the contract.

It seems that more lawsuits are being filed by agents who feel their clients have treated them unfairly by breaking a contract. An agent usually puts a lot of hard work into helping a client buy or sell a home. Therefore, it is very important that you hire an agent you are sure you want to work with for a while. If the agent seems like somebody you might "bump heads" with in the future, you might want to reconsider your choice of agents.

By using one of the above methods you should be able to find a good real estate agent. Your decision could be a critical determining point of whether or not you are treated in the manner you deserve.

Looking For Someone to Sell Your Home?

Try Going to an Open House

By Denny R. Stephens

You have made the decision to sell your house. As important as that decision is, the next most important is selecting a real estate agent who will not just list your home with the agency and place a sign out front. You want someone who will represent your home in the best possible way.

One way to find a good agent is to go to open houses for homes that are for sale. Start your quest for an agent by following some of these handy guidelines.

First, look though the real estate ads in your local paper for houses that are comparable to yours. Look for houses of similar building style, square footage, age and even location. Don't forget to look at houses for sale in your own neighborhood.

When you have a list of homes and their open house dates and times, begin your search. When you drive up to the open house, note how well is it advertised. Were there well-placed signs that led easily to the open house? Are the hours and dates posted? Do you see little touches like balloons, tasteful banners—anything that invites the attentions of prospective buyers? A house for sale always makes its first impression from the street.

When you walk inside the front door, note some of the following. What aromas greet you? Maybe a soft hint of vanilla, perhaps even the aroma of cinnamon wafting from the kitchen. Aroma helps set the mood and can make people think of the house they are entering as a home.

At this point, the owners of the house should not be there; this is easiest for all parties concerned. Take a good look around. Is there a guest register for your name and address? This serves two purposes. It gives the realtor a potential customer list and it registers everyone that enters the home. The real estate agent also should have instructed the sellers of the home to either hide, lock away, or take with them any small, valuable items. People will be looking through closet and cupboards. If a number of people are wandering around, an agent can't keep track of them all.

As you go through the house, look for informational prompts on the particular room you are in, the house itself, or the area it is located in. These can be small signs that tell the prospective buyers about the local school system or that the central air conditioning unit is new and still under warranty. If the agent is busy talking to, and keeping track of several people throughout the house, these signs give key information to the buyers without the agent.

The agent should have an information center set up somewhere near the starting or ending point of the house tour. This should display vital information about the house such as the square footage, utility expenses, asking price, maybe even a floor plan or sales flyers, etc. Also look for information about the various types of financing available and the different lending institutions.

Last, is the agent attentive and friendly? Remember, you are looking for someone to market your home effectively. Has the agent assembled an inviting and informative open house? Does he or she seem glad you have stopped in to look around? Remember, you are using the open house as part of an interview process. If you are impressed with the capability and demeanor of the agent in representing other homes, chances are that agent will do a good job in the marketing of your home. Happy agent hunting.